Guitar Sight-Reading

Introductory Single Line Exercises

by

Paulo Oliveira

©2022 FretZone Music Publishing

Nashville, TN - USA

Guitar Sight-Reading

Introductory Single Line Exercises

by Paulo Oliveira

© 2022 by FretZone Music Publishing

Nashville, TN

ISBN: 978-1-7374515-1-8

Table of Contents

Introduction

This book was written for guitar students who want to develop their sight reading skills. This material focuses on single-line exercises in first position (first four frets), including the use of open strings. However, the student can read most of the exercises all the way up to the fifth position (frets 5 to 8). Basic single-line sight reading can be a lonely and unexciting task at times. For this reason, this book includes chord changes for the first two units and duos in units three and four. This will allow students to play with their teachers and peers, and will help them develop ensemble playing and sight reading skills at the same time. When working with a partner it is important to switch parts in order to get more practice out of the exercises. At the end of the book, I am including some basic chord shapes to help students develop their vocabulary of chords. That way, the student will be able to provide an accompaniment part for the single-line exercises.

The content is divided into five units:

- The first unit focuses on the top three strings and simple rhythms.
- The second unit introduces the bass notes, and includes subdivisions up to eight notes.
- The third unit contains eighteen duos, with the use of key signatures and rhythmic materials presented in the first two units of the book.
- The fourth unit is divided into six rhythmic groups, each of them introducing different rhythmic patterns. The first example of each group presents the rhythms in a single-line exercise that can be sung or played using one single note on the guitar. The goal of the first exercise of each group is to focus solely on rhythm. Each rhythmic group is followed by three duos that are based on those specific rhythms.
- The fifth unit presents selected chord shapes for the accompaniment of the exercises.

Acknowledgments

I would like to give a special thanks to José Ricardo for his editorial assistance, and for allowing me to include some of his duets in this publication (Duos 31 through 36). To Amorim Lopes, for his beautiful artwork on the cover, and also my students and colleagues at Belmont University for inspiring me to make this book a reality.

Practice Tips

The key to improving your sight reading is to practice consistently, ideally every day. Twenty to thirty minutes of daily practice on sight reading will give you great results after a semester. You should read the exercises slowly, and speed them up little by little. If you find passages that are more challenging, make sure to isolate them and work on them separately. However, you do not need to repeat the exercise or passage to the point of memorization. The goal is to be able to play with fluidity, but without memorizing it. In order to develop this fluidity, your eyes should always be looking at a few notes ahead of the note you are playing.

Left Hand Fingerings and String Notation

Left Hand Fingers:

1 - Index
2 - Middle
3 - Ring
4 - Pinkie

Strings:

E   B   G   D   A   E

①   ②   ③   ④   ⑤   ⑥

Open strings:

0 ⓪

Unit 1: Strings 1, 2 and 3

"The level of achievement that we have at anything,

is a reflection of how well, we were able to focus on it."

Steve Vai

Notes on the First String

Notes on the Second String

From First to Second String

Ode to Joy

Beethoven
(1770-1827)

Imitation for Three

This piece is an imitation for up to three guitarists.
Each new player begins when the previous player gets to the asterisk (*)
Play it twice through without stoping.

1.Ties, dots and Half-Note Rests

2. Introducing F# and C#

Sharp (#) : Raises the note a half step, up one fret.
The note will remain as a sharp for the entire measure, unless you see a natural sign (♮).

Natural Sign (♮): Cancels the effect of sharps and flats, the note becomes natural.
E.g. F# becomes F

3. Introducing Eb and Ab

Flat (b) : Lowers the note a half step, down one fret.
The note will remain as a flat for the entire measure, unless you see a natural sign (♮).

4. Combining Sharps and Flats

5. Blues with Flats and Sharps

6. Syncopation and Quarter-Note Rests

7. Syncopation and Accidentals

8. Syncopation and Accidentals

Introducing the Third String

1

2

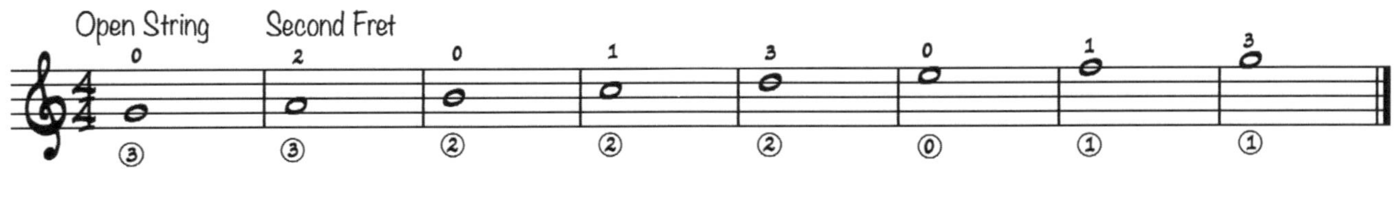

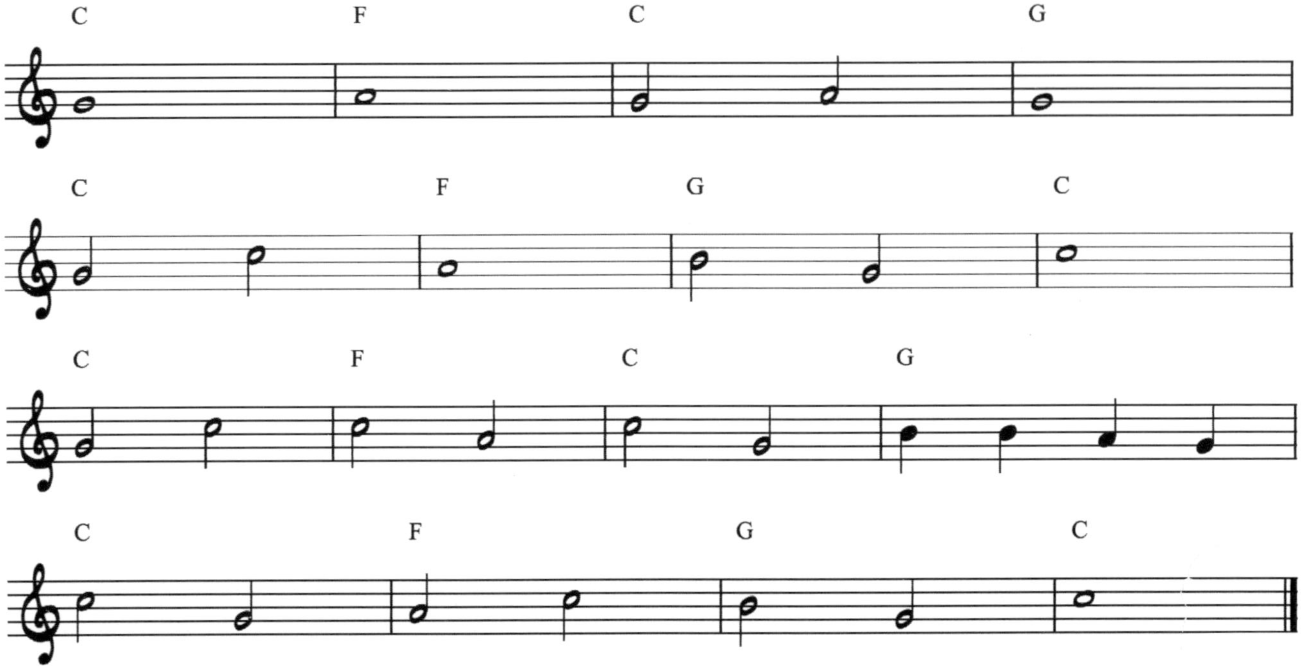

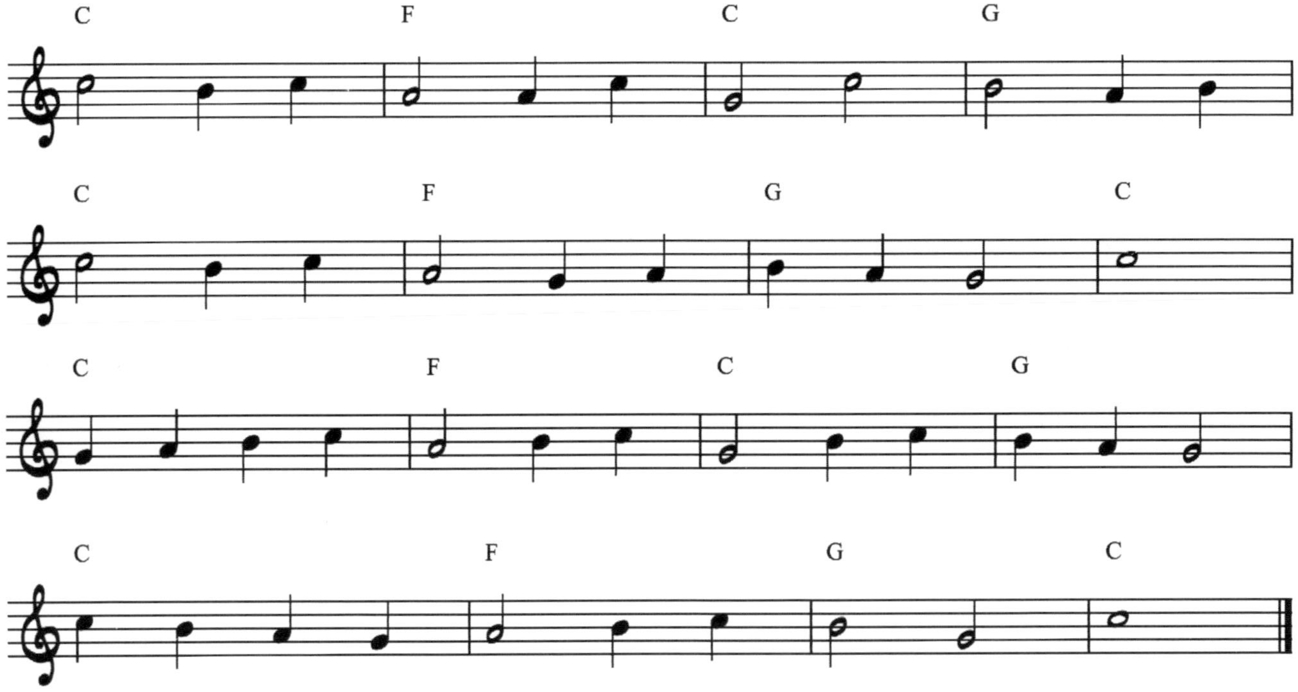

3. Introducing Bb and ¾ Time Signature

4

5

CMaj7   Dm7   G7   CMaj7   Dm7   G7
CMaj7   Dm7   G7   CMaj7   Am7   Bb7   G7
C6   Dm7   G7   C6   Dm7   G13
CMaj7   Dm7   G7   CMaj7   FMaj7   C6
FMaj7   CMaj7
Fm7   D9   G7
CMaj7   Dm7   G7   CMaj7   Dm7   G13
Am7   Dm7   G13   C6   Fm7   C6

6

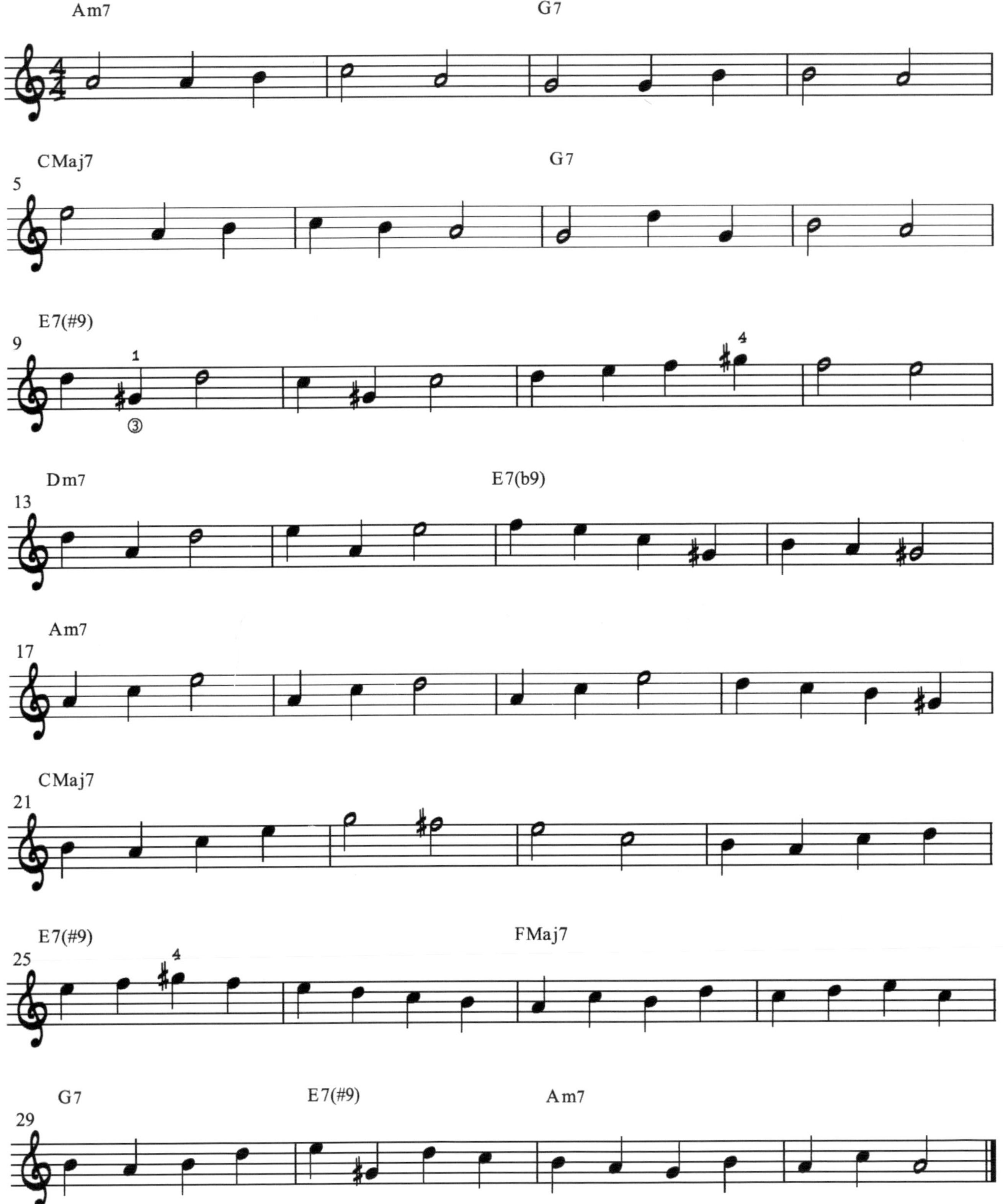

7

CMaj7
FMaj7
CMaj7
FMaj7
CMaj7
FMaj7
B♭Maj7
Gsus9
G7
CMaj7
FMaj7
CMaj7
FMaj7
C6(9)
FMaj7
B♭Maj7
C7
FMaj7
B♭7
CMaj7
C9
FMaj7
B♭7
Am7
D9
G7
C6(9)
Gsus9
FMaj7
CMaj7

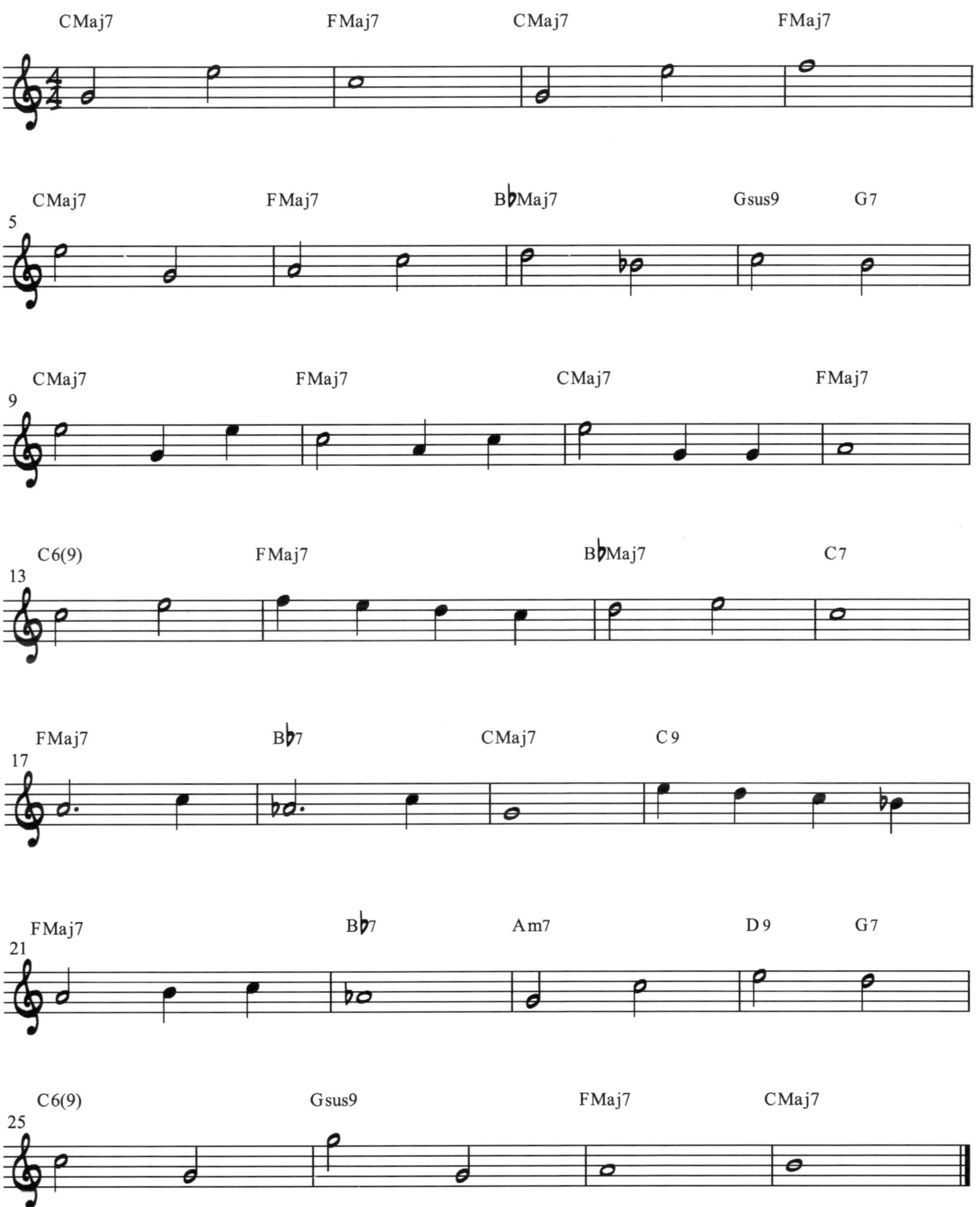

8

9

FMaj7   Gm7   C7   FMaj7   Gm7   C 9
FMaj7   Gm7   C 9   FMaj7   Dm7   E♭6   C7
FMaj7   Gm7   C 9   FMaj7   Gm7   C 9
FMaj7   Gm7   C   FMaj7   B♭Maj7   FMaj7
B♭Maj7   FMaj7
B♭m7   G7   C 9
FMaj7   Gm7   C 9   FMaj7   Gm7   C 9
FMaj7   Gm7   C 9   FMaj7   B♭Maj7   FMaj7

10

F7
Bb7
F7
Bb7
F7
C7
Bb7
F7
F7
Bb7
F7
Bb7
F7
C7
Bb7
F7
F7
Bb7
F7
Bb7
F7
C7
Bb7
F7

11

12

Dm7
Gm6
A7
Dm7
Dm7
Gm6
A7
Dm7
Gm6
Dm7
A7
Dm7
Gm6
Dm7
E7
A7(b13)
Dm7
Gm6
A7(b13)
Dm7
Dm7
Gm6
A7(b13)
Dm7

13

14

FMaj7
BbMaj7
C 9
FMaj7
Dm7
Am7
BbMaj7
C 9
FMaj7
F13
BbMaj7
Bbm7
FMaj7
C 9
FMaj7
F 7
Bb
FMaj7
BbMaj7
G 13
Gm7
C 9
FMaj7
F 7
BbMaj7
Bbm7
FMaj7
C 9
F 6

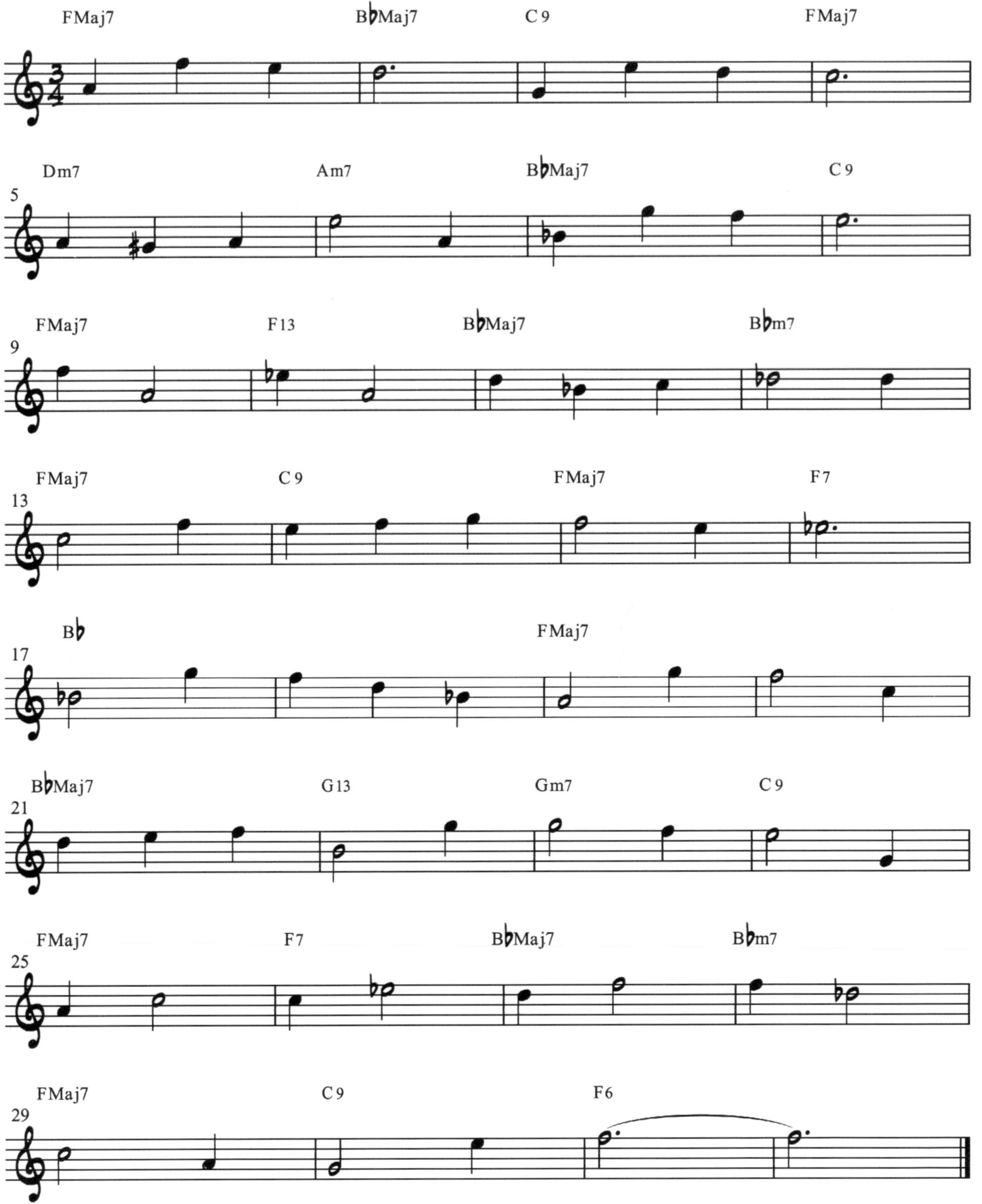

15

Em7
CMaj7
Em7
D7
Am7
GMaj7
Am7
Em7
Am7
GMaj7
Am7
B7
Em
Am
D
Em
CMaj7
Bm7
Em7
Em7
Am7
D7
Em7
Am7
Bm7
Em7

16

CMaj7   Dm9   G13   CMaj7   Dm7   G13
CMaj7   Dm9   G13   C6   Am7   B♭Maj7   G13
CMaj7   Dm9   G13   CMaj7   Dm9   G13
CMaj7   Dm9   G13   CMaj7   Fm7   C6
FMaj7   CMaj7
Fm7   D9   G13
C6(9)   Dm9   G13   C6(9)   Dm9   G13
CMaj7   Dm9   G13   A♭Maj7   CMaj7

17

Bbm7
Ebm6
Bbm7
GbMaj7
F7(b13)
Bbm7
Ebm7
Bbm7
GbMaj7
F7(b13)
Bbm7

Unit II : Strings 4, 5 and 6

"A little progress each day adds up to big results."

Satya Nani

Notes on the Fourth String

3

F6
B♭Maj7
C9
F6
Dm9
Am7
B♭Maj7
C9
F6
F13
B♭6(9)
B♭m7
F6
C9
F6
F13
B♭6(9)
F13
F7(b13)
B♭Maj7
G13
Gm7
C7
F6
F13
B♭6(9)
B♭m6
F6
C9
F6

4

5

CMaj7 Dm7 G13 CMaj7 Dm7 G13
CMaj7 Dm7 G13 C6 Am7 BbMaj7 G13
CMaj7 Dm7 G13 C6 Dm7 G13
CMaj7 Dm7 G13 CMaj7 FMaj7 CMaj7
FMaj7 F6 C6 Gb7(#11)
Fm7 D9 G13
C6 Dm7 G13 C6 Dm7 G13
C6 A7(b13) Dm7 G13 C6 Fm7 C6

6

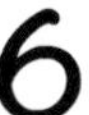

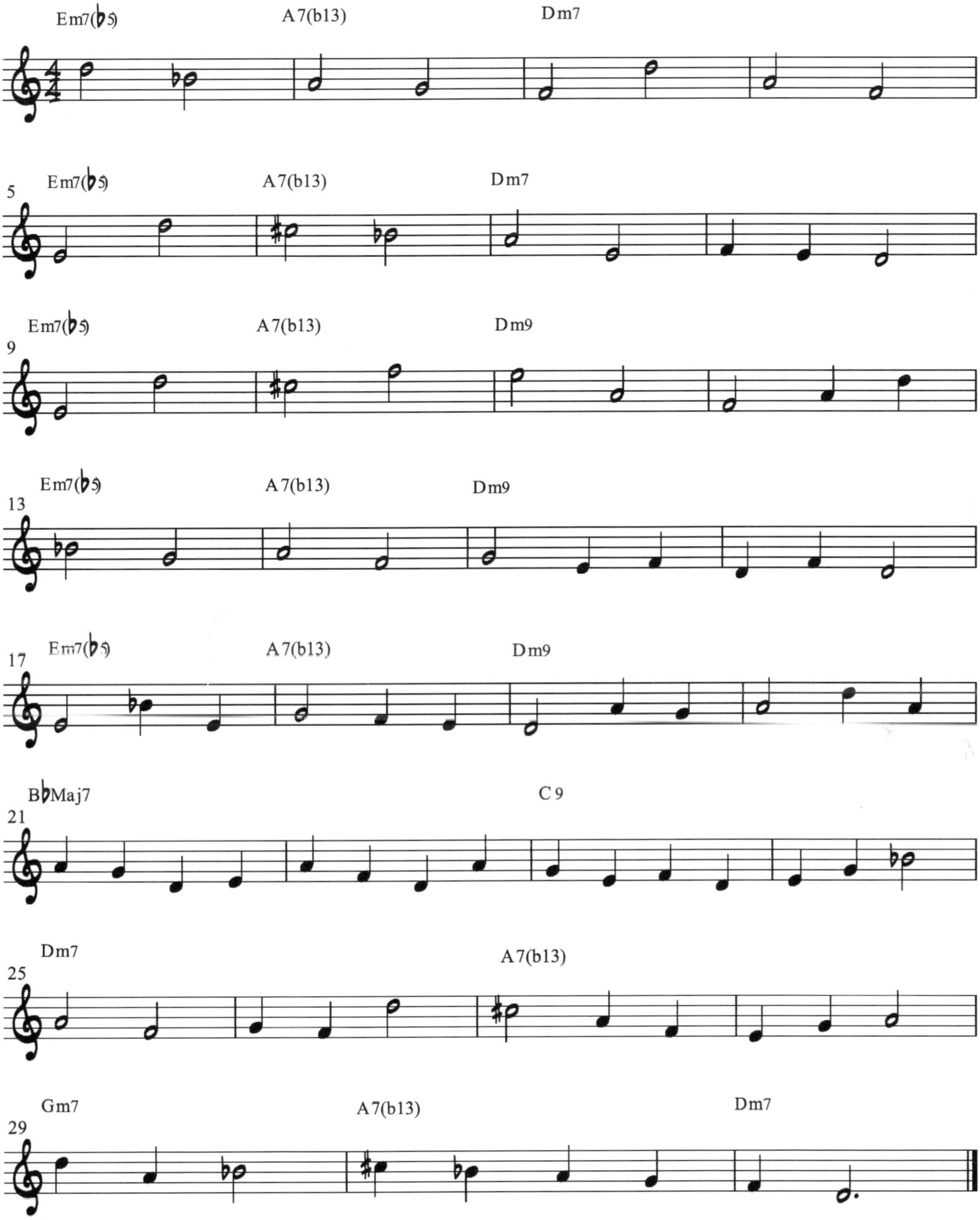
Em7(b5)
A7(b13)
Dm7
5
Em7(b5)
A7(b13)
Dm7
9
Em7(b5)
A7(b13)
Dm9
13
Em7(b5)
A7(b13)
Dm9
17
Em7(b5)
A7(b13)
Dm9
21
BbMaj7
C9
25
Dm7
A7(b13)
29
Gm7
A7(b13)
Dm7

7

CMaj7
FMaj7
CMaj7
FMaj7
CMaj7
FMaj7
B♭Maj7
Gsus9
CMaj7
FMaj7
CMaj7
FMaj7
CMaj7
FMaj7
B♭Maj7
C9
FMaj7
B♭7
CMaj7
C9
FMaj7
B♭7
Am7
D9
G13
CMaj7
Gsus9
B♭Maj7
CMaj7

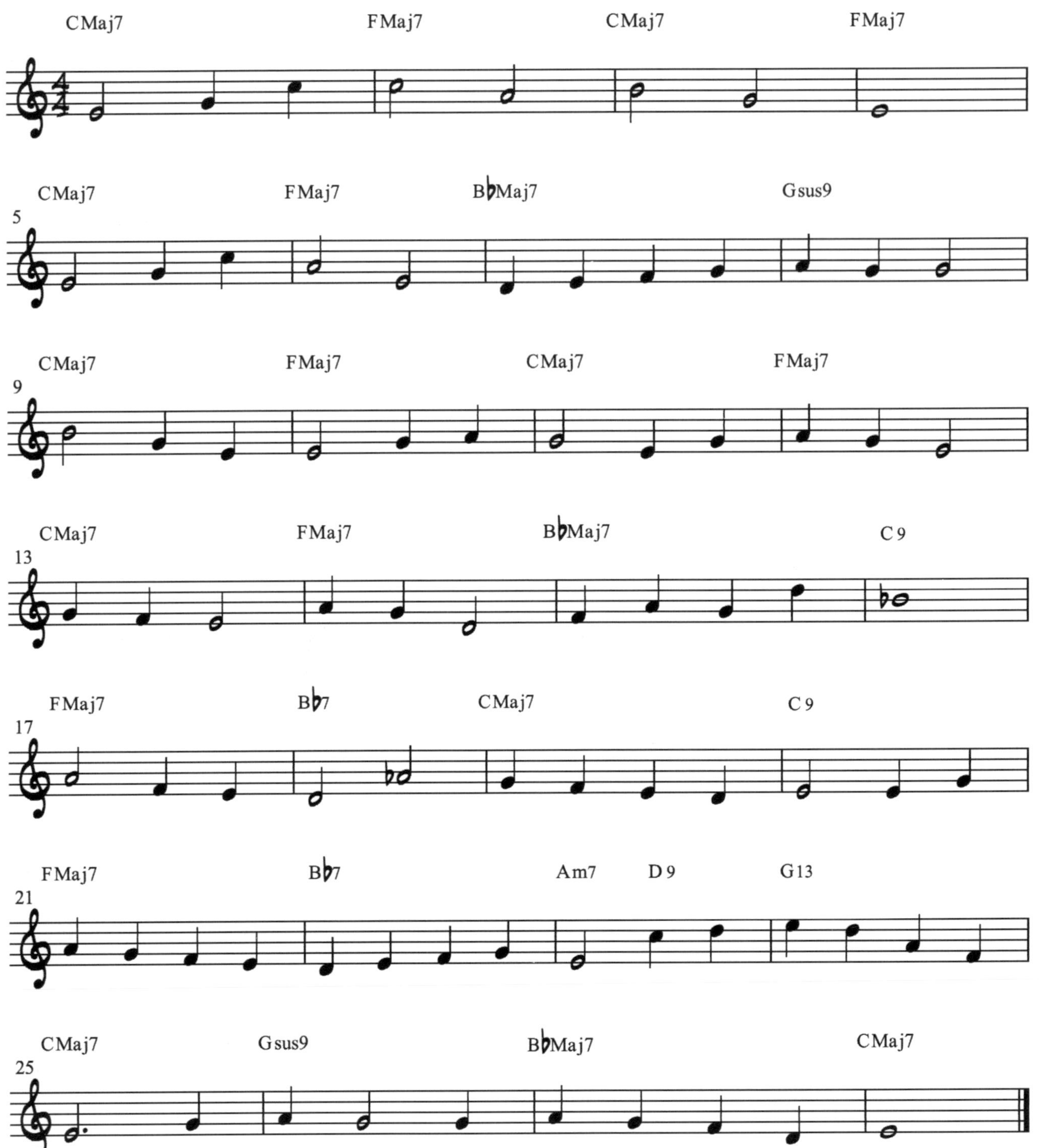

8

9

FMaj7   Gm7   C 9   FMaj7   Gm7   C 9
FMaj7   Gm7   C 9   FMaj7   Dm7   E♭Maj7   C 9
FMaj7   Gm7   C 9   Dm7   Gm7   C 9
F6   Gm7   C 9   B♭Maj7   B 9
B♭Maj7   C 9
B♭m7   G13   C7(#9)
FMaj7   Gm7   C 9   FMaj7   Gm7   C 9
FMaj7   D7(#9)   Gm7   C7(b9)   FMaj7

Notes on the Fifth String

3

CMaj7   FMaj7   CMaj7   FMaj7
CMaj7   FMaj7   BbMaj7   Gsus9   G7
CMaj7   FMaj7   CMaj7   FMaj7
CMaj7   FMaj7   BbMaj7   C9
FMaj7   Bb7   CMaj7   C9
FMaj7   Bb7   Am7   D7
CMaj7   Gsus9   G7   FMaj7   C6

4

5

6

FMaj7 Gm C 9 FMaj7 Gm C 9
FMaj7 Gm C 9 FMaj7 Dm E♭Maj7 C7
FMaj7 Gm C 9 FMaj7 Gm C 9
FMaj7 Gm C 9 FMaj7 B♭m7 FMaj7
B♭Maj7 FMaj7
B♭m7 G7 C 9
FMaj7 Gm7 C 9 FMaj7 Gm7 C 9
FMaj7 Gm C 9 FMaj7 B♭m7 FMaj7

Notes on the Sixth String

3

4

F
Bb
C7
F
Dm
Am
Bb
C7
F
F7
Bb
Bbm
F
C7
F
F7
Bb
F
Bb
G7
Gm7
C7
F
F7
Bb
Bbm
F
C7
F

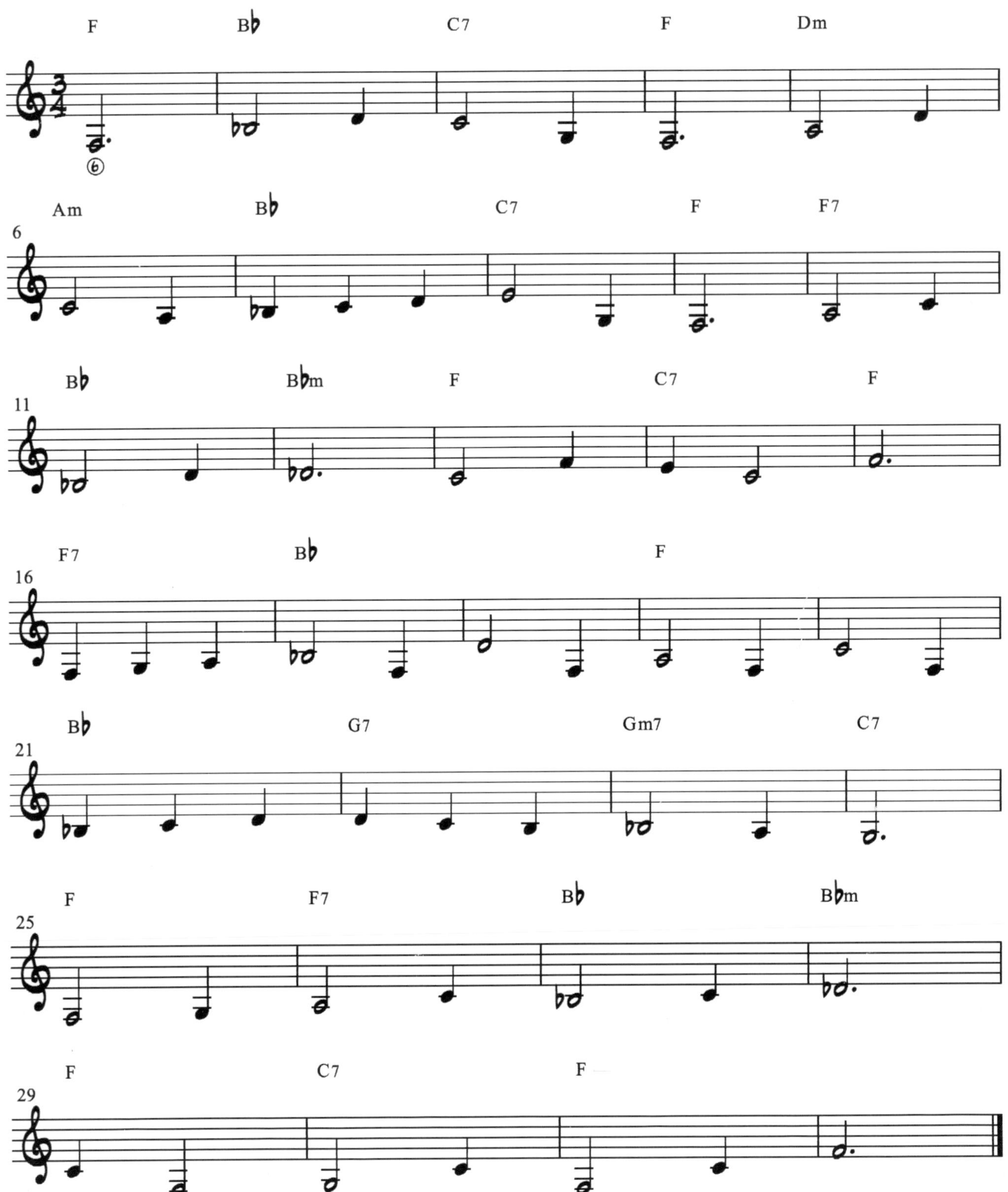

5

Em9
CMaj7
Em9
D6(9)
Am7
GMaj7
Am7
E7(#9)
Am7
GMaj7
Am7
B7(b9)
E7(#9)
Am7
D6(9)
Em9
CMaj7
Bm7
Em9
E7(b9)
Am7
D6(9)
Em9
Am7
Bm7
E7(#9)

6

BbMaj7
Dm7
EbMaj7
Cm7
EbMaj7
F7
BbMaj7
Dm7
Gm7
EbMaj7
BbMaj7
Cm7
AbMaj7
F7
BbMaj7
Dm7
EbMaj7
BbMaj7
Cm7
F7
EbMaj7
BbMaj7
Bass Notes

Unit III : Duo Series (Simple Rhythms)

"A person who never made a mistake never tried anything new."

Albert Einstein

Duo n. 1

Duo n. 2

Duo n. 3

The sharp sign (#) at the beginning of each line means that all "Fs" should be sharp, on every octave, unless there is natural sign.

Duo n. 4

Duo n. 5

Duo n. 6

Duo n. 7

Duo n. 8

After the statement of the melody students can improvise over the chords and bass line.

Duo n. 9 - Good King Wenceslas

Duo n. 10 - Deck the Halls

Starting on Duo. 10 you will find the addition of the dotted quarter note, which is equivalent to three eight notes.

Duo n. 11 - God Rest Ye Merry, Gentlemen

Duo n. 12 - O Come all Ye Faithful

Duo n. 13 - See, Amid the Winter Snow

Duo n. 14 - While Shepherds Watched

Duo n. 15 - Unto us a Boy is Born

Duo n. 16 - It Came Upon the Midnight Clear

Duo n. 17 - Joy to the World

Duo n. 18 - Hark! The Herald Angels Sing

Unit III : Duo Series (Rhythmic Groups)

"The beautiful thing about learning is that no one can take it away from you."

B. B. King

Rhythmic Group A

Duo n. 19

Duo n. 20

Duo n. 21

Rhythmic Group B

Duo n. 22

Duo n. 23

Tambora: lightly hit the bridge of the guitar with the side of your thumb creating a percussive drum sound.

Duo n. 24

Lightly hit the bridge (right hand) or the side of the guitar (left hand) creating a distinct percussive sounds.

Rhythmic Group C

Duo n. 25

Duo n. 26

Duo n. 27

Rhythmic Group D

The measures that say "same rhythm" present the exact same rhythm as the measure immediately before it, but with a different type of notation.

Duo n. 28

Duo n. 29

Swing
Em7(♭5)
A7
Dm7
Gm7
C7
Fmaj7
Em7(♭5) A7
Dm7
Gm7
B♭7
Em7(♭5) A7
Dm7
G7
Em7(♭5)
A7
Dm7

Duo n. 30

Bossa
Cm7
Fm7
Dm7(b5)
G7
Cm7
Ebm7
Ab7
Dbmaj7
Dm7(b5)
G7
Cm7
Dm7(b5) G7
Cm7

Rhythmic Group E

Duo n. 31

*This duo works better when played in third position, frets 3-6.

Duo n. 32

Duo n. 32

Duo n. 33

Duo n. 33

Rhythmic Group F

Duo n. 34

Duo n. 35

Duo n. 35

Duo n. 36

Duo n. 36

Rhythmic Group G

Duo n. 37

Duo n. 38

Duo n. 38

Duo n. 39

Duo n. 39

Unit V: Selected Chord Shapes

> "The way to get started is to quit talking and begin doing."
>
> Walt Disney

Selected Chord Shapes

This unit contains a few selected seventh and sixth chords and some of the most common shapes with extensions including 9 and 13.

They are divided into three groups: root on the 6th string, root on the 5th string, and root on the 4th string.

These shapes can be transposed chromatically to any key.

The letter "R" represents the root and the numbers inside the circles indicate the interval of the note in relation to the root.

Chords with the root on the 6th string

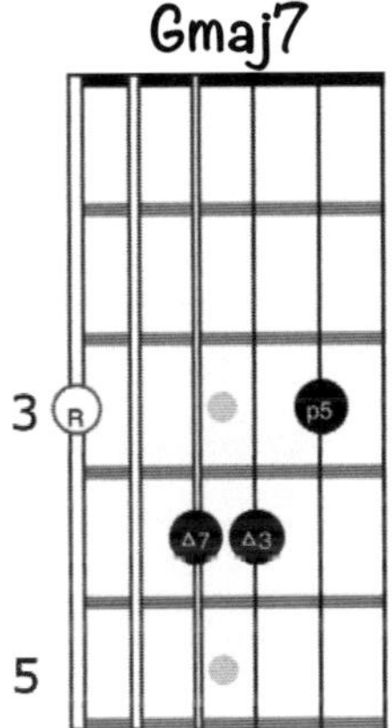

Gmaj7

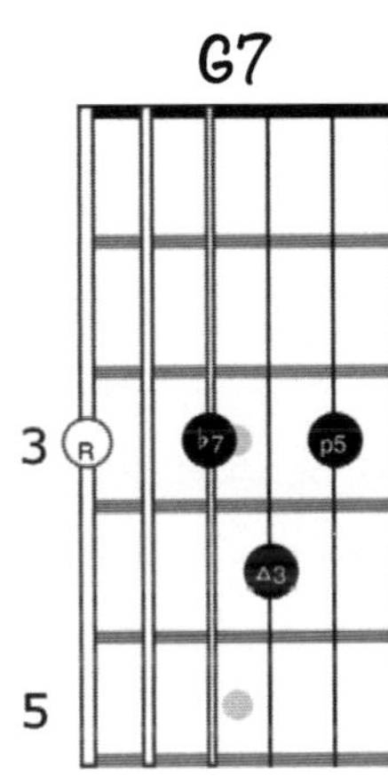

G7

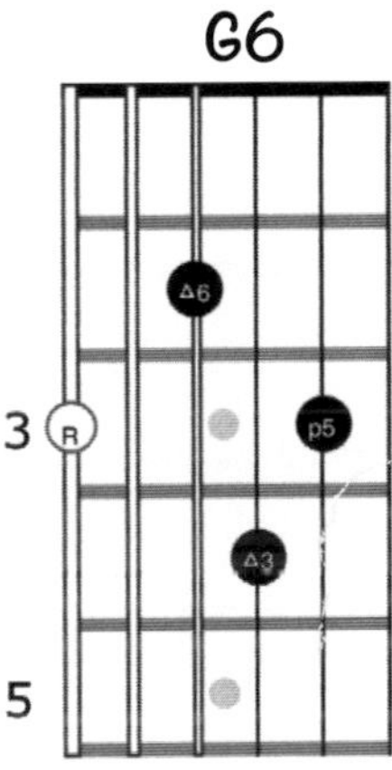

G6

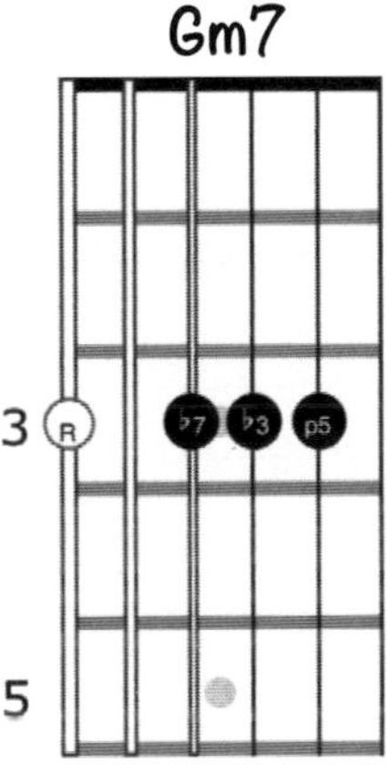

Gm7

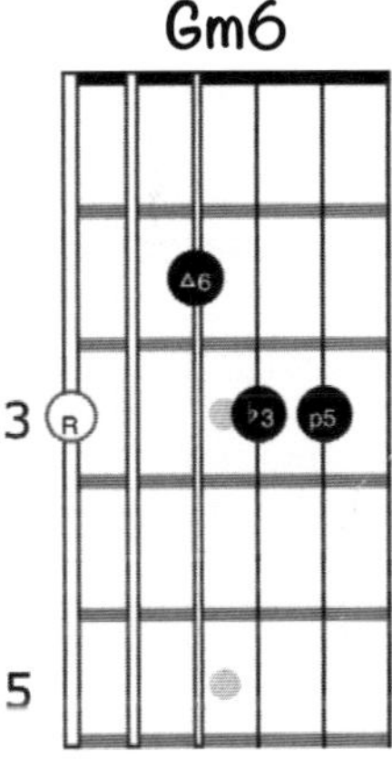

Gm6

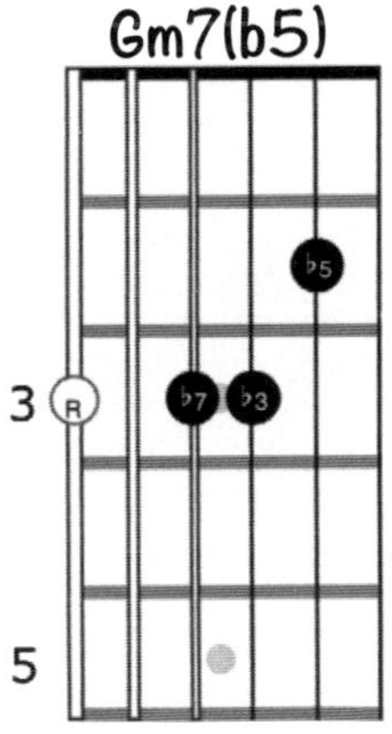

Gm7(b5)

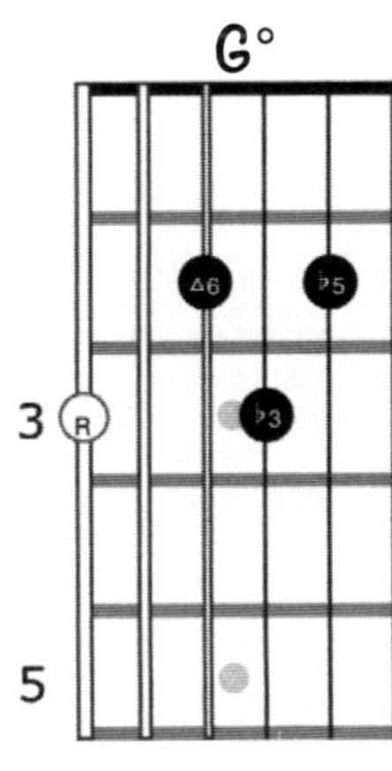

G°

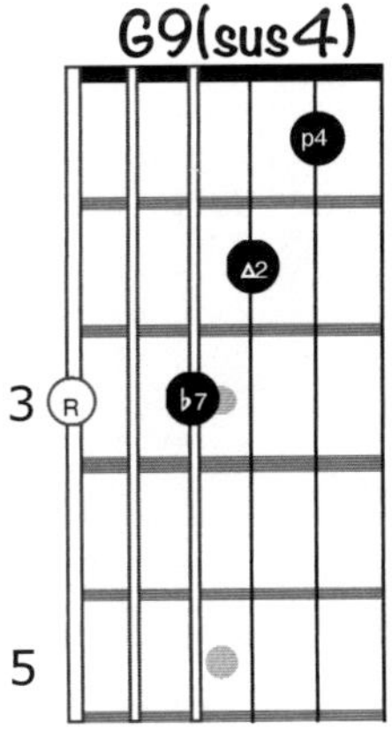

G9(sus4)

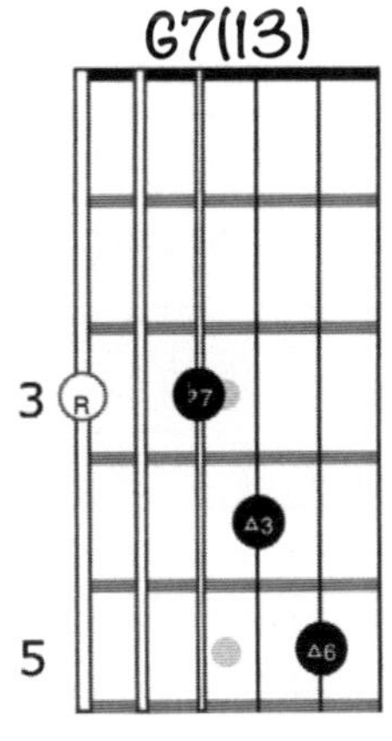

G7(13)

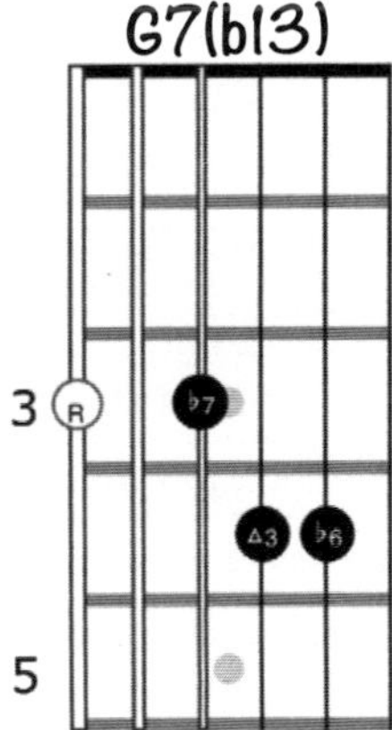

G7(b13)

Chords with the root on the 5th string

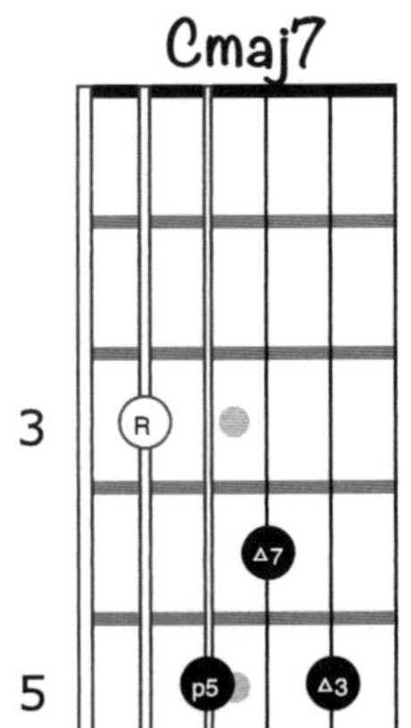

Cmaj7

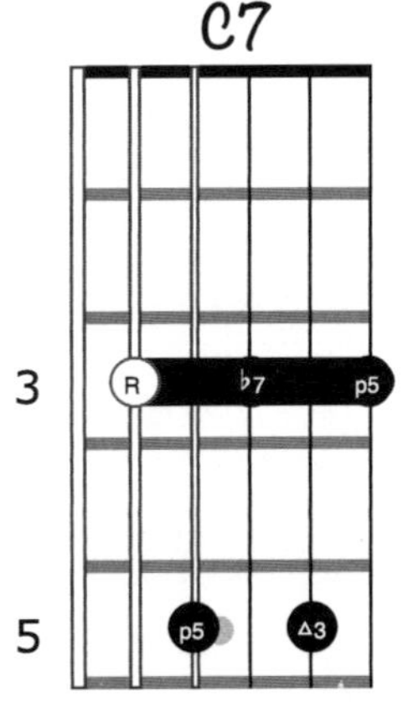

C7

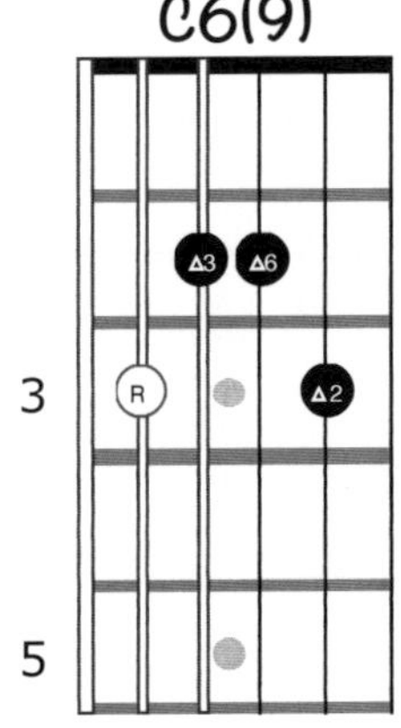

C6(9)

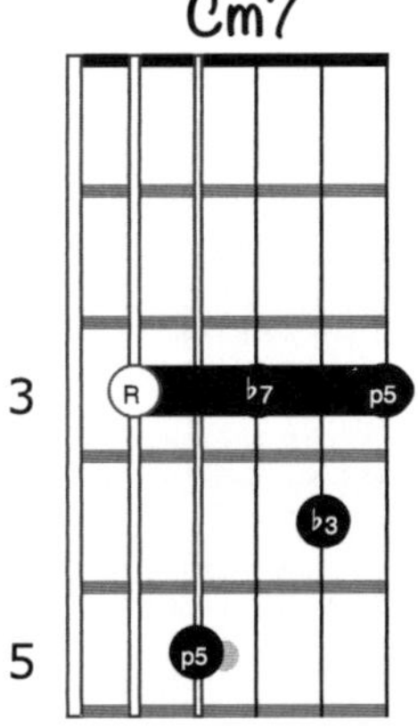

Cm7

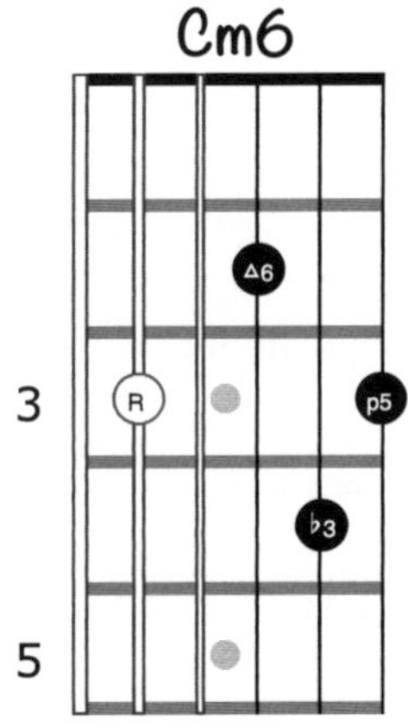

Cm6

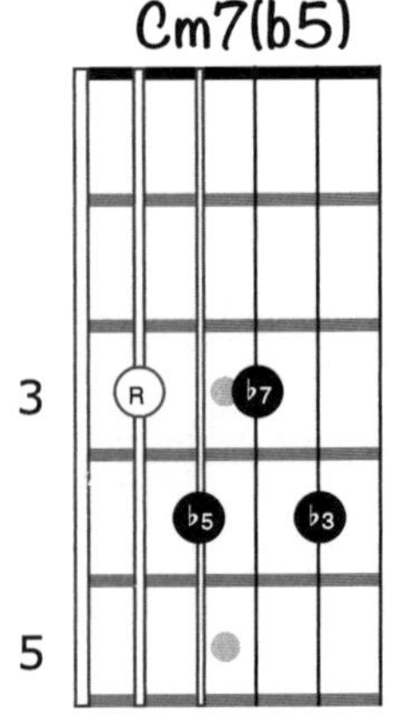

Cm7(b5)

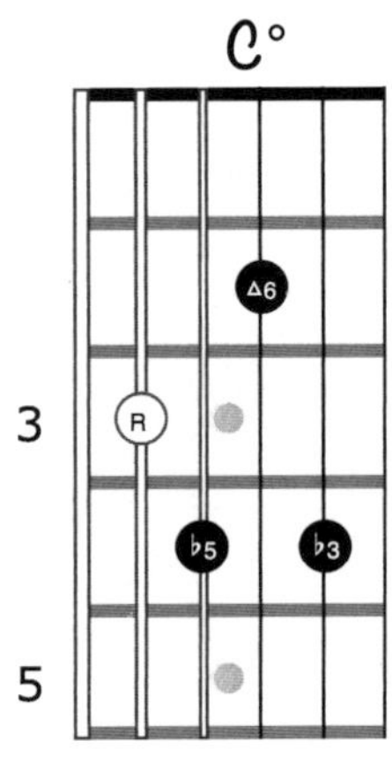

C°

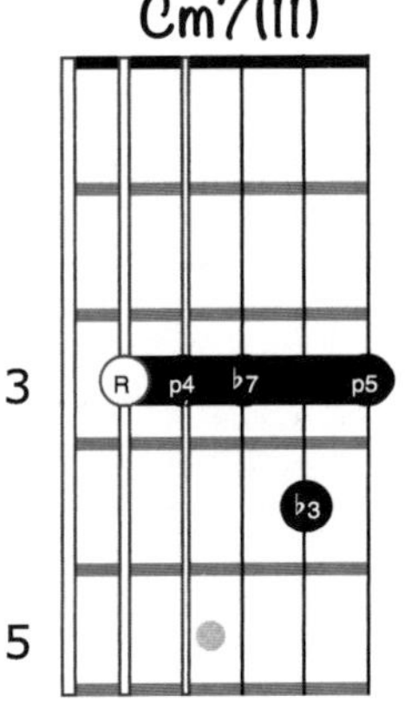

Cm7(11)

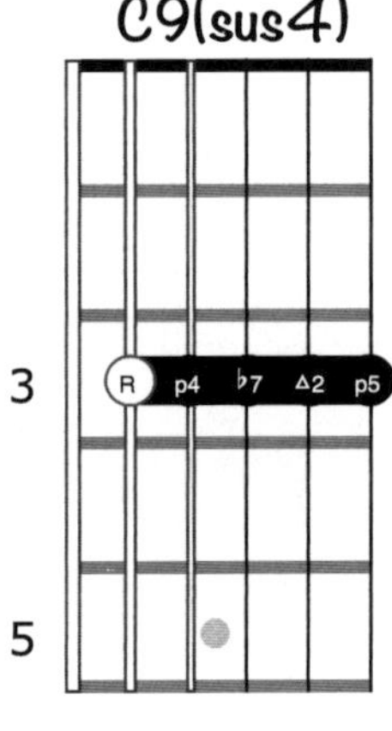

C9(sus4)

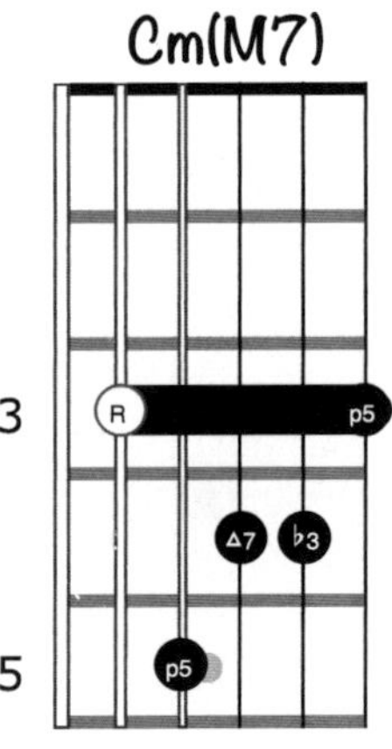

Cm(M7)

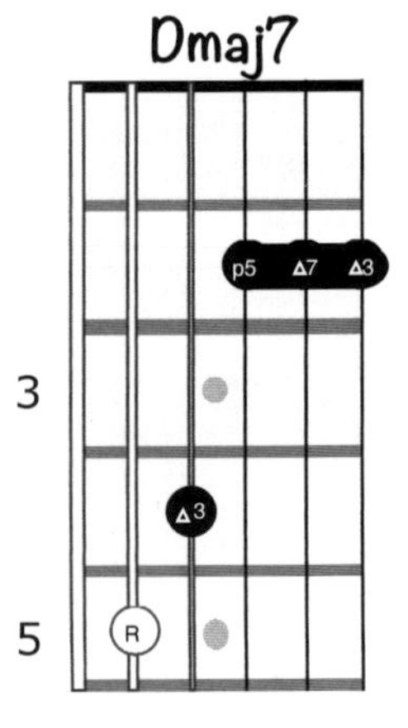

Dmaj7

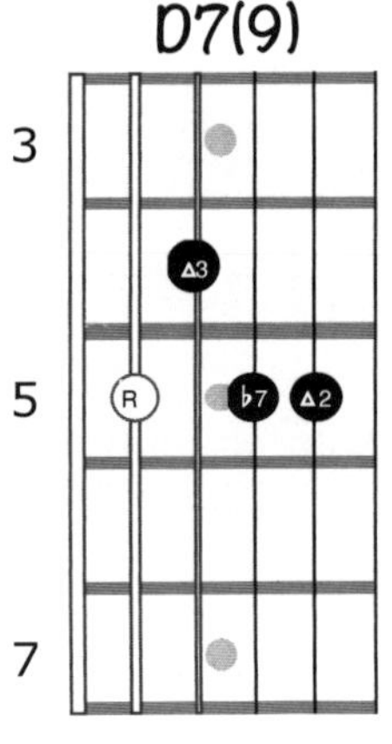

D7(9)

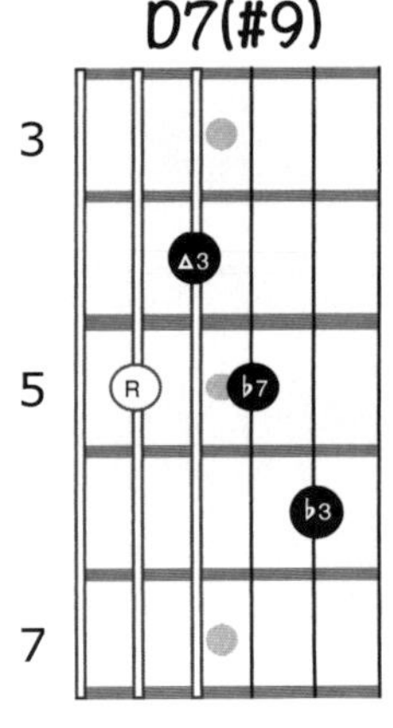

D7(#9)

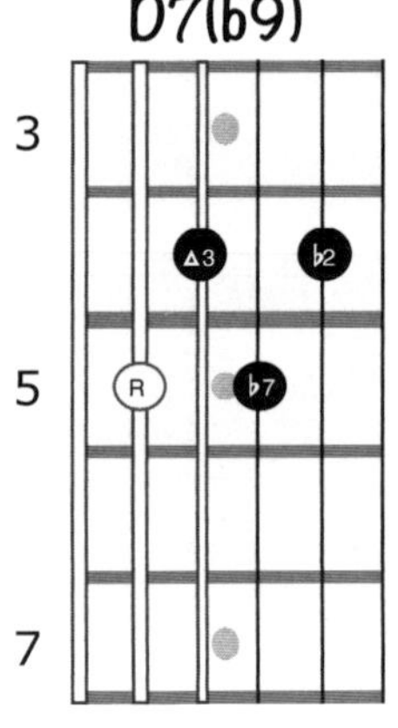

D7(b9)

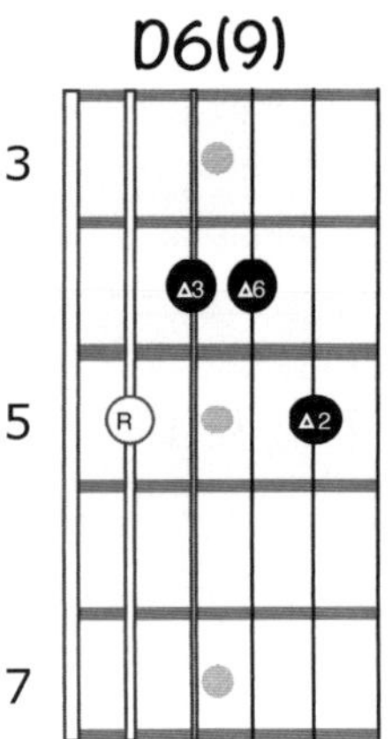

D6(9)

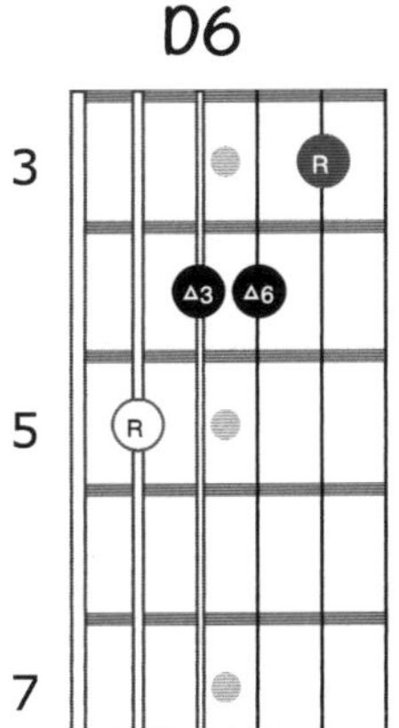

D6

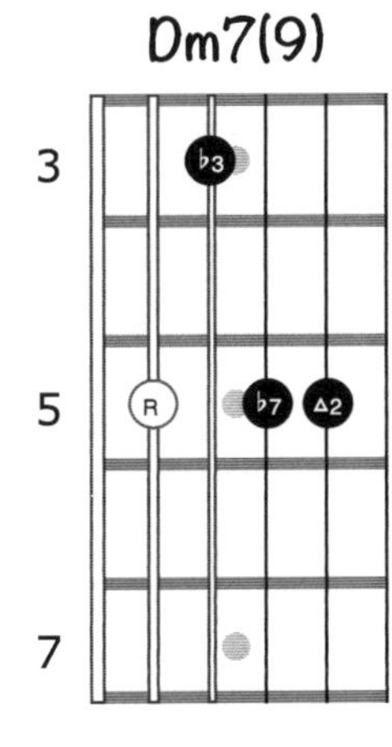

Dm7(9)

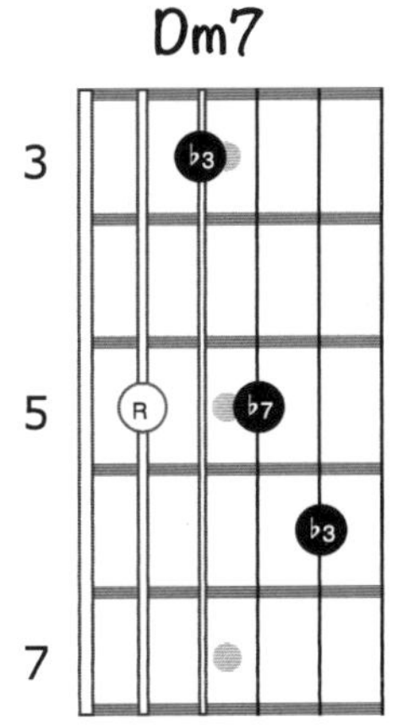

Dm7

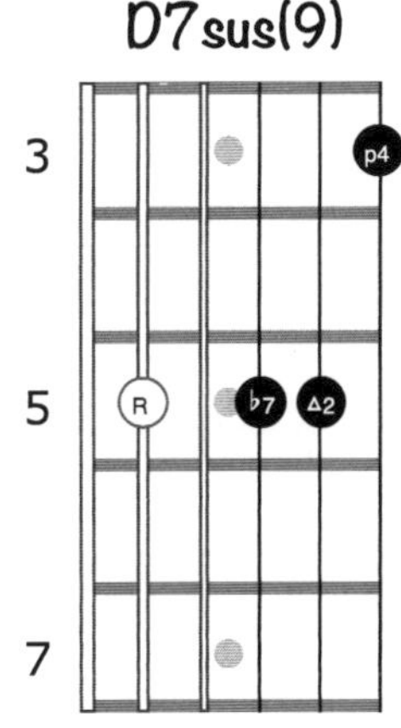

D7sus(9)

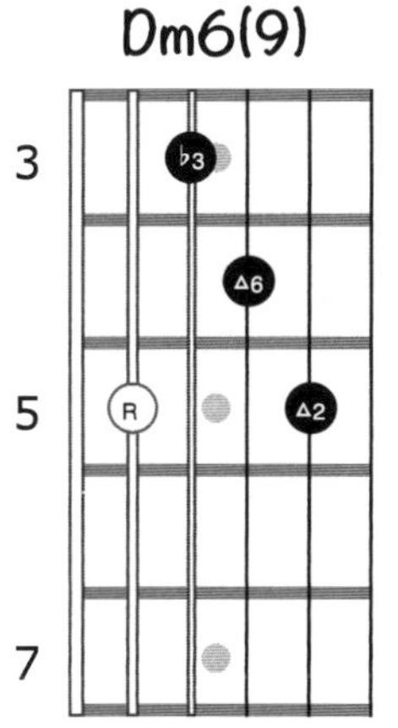

Dm6(9)

Chords with the root on the 4th string

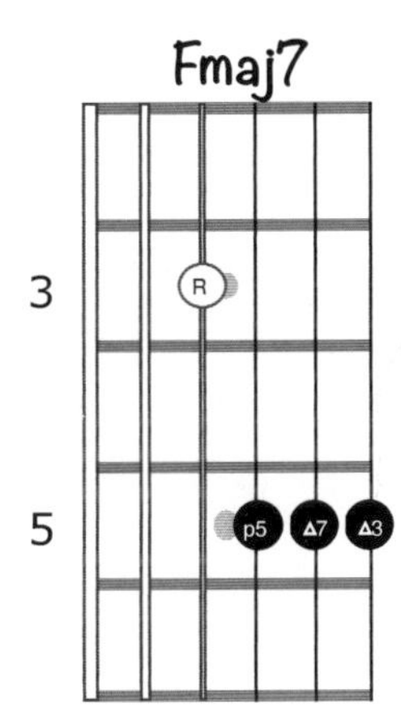

Fmaj7

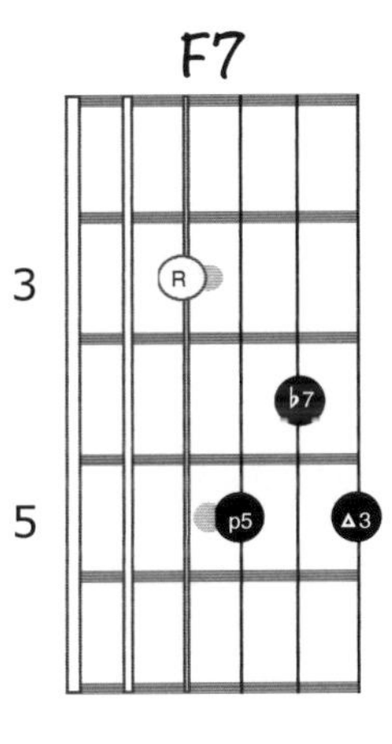

F7

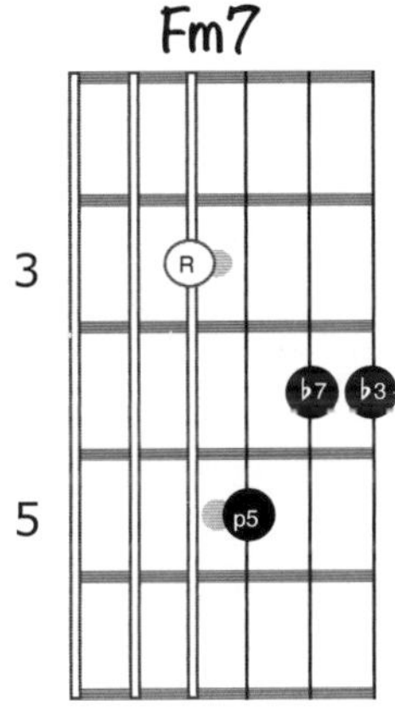

Fm7

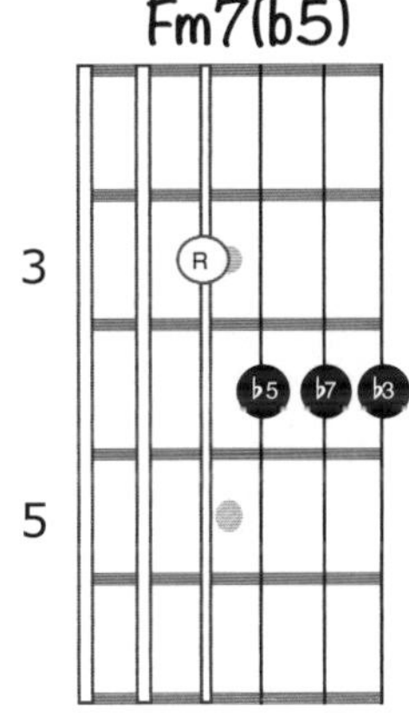

Fm7(b5)

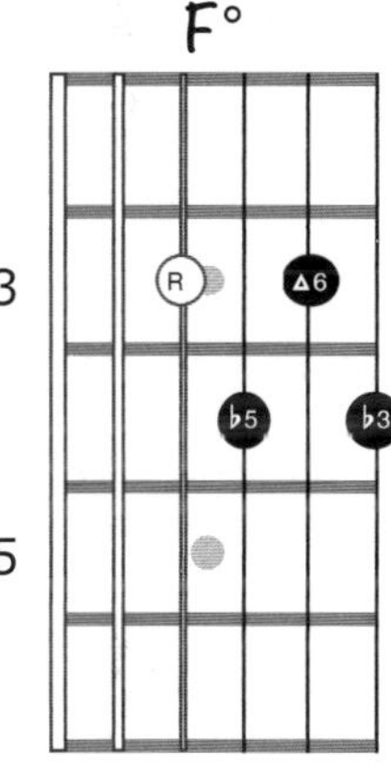

F°

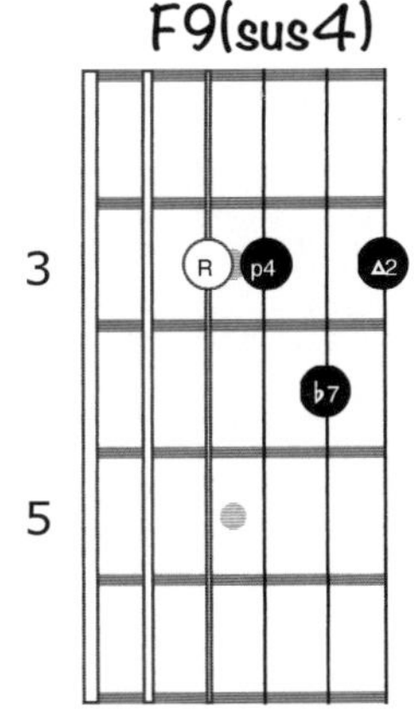

F9(sus4)

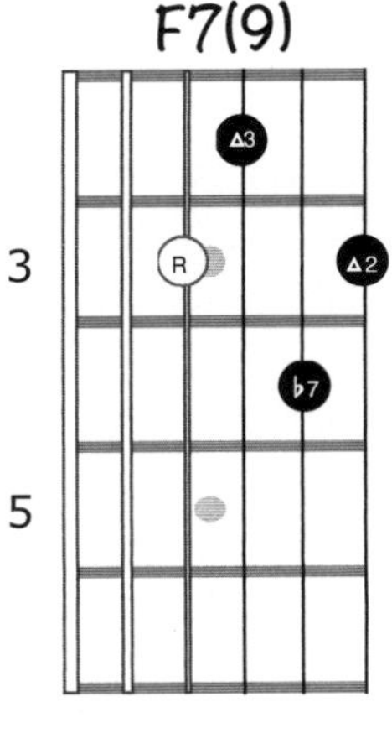

F7(9)

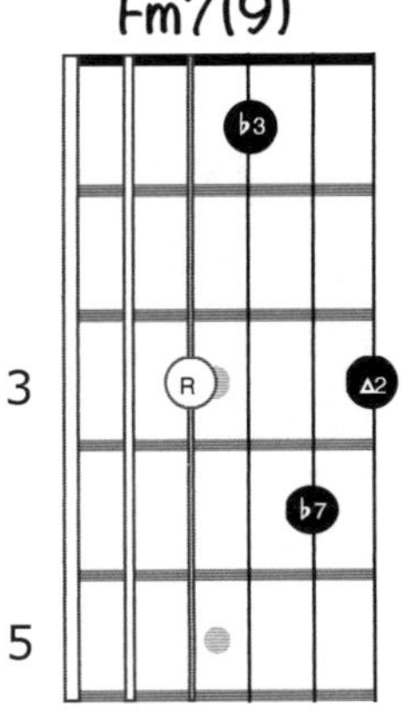

Fm7(9)

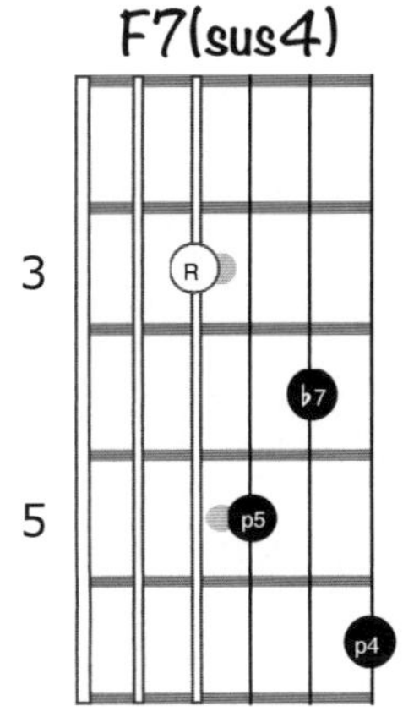

F7(sus4)

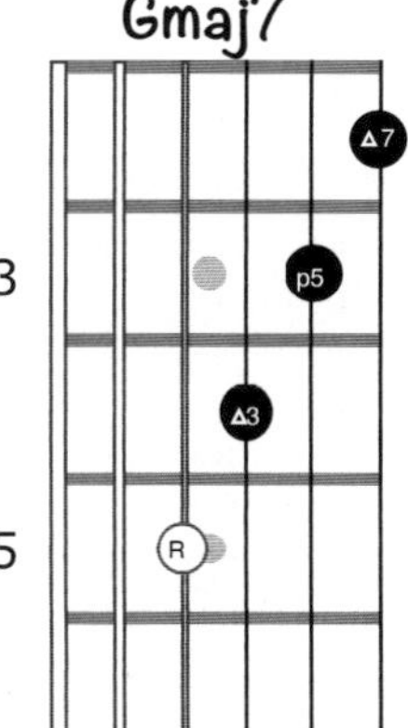

Gmaj7